A Status of Adivasis/Indigenous Peoples Land Series – 2

ORISSA

Kundan Kumar
with P R Choudhury, Soumen Sarangi,
Pradeep Mishra and Sricharan Behera

A Status of Adivasis/Indigenous Peoples Land Series – 2 : ORISSA
Kundan Kumar *with* P R Choudhury, Soumen Sarangi, Pradeep Mishra and Sricharan Behera

First Published, 2011

ISBN 978-93-5002-122-4

Published by
AAKAR BOOKS
28 E Pocket IV, Mayur Vihar Phase I, Delhi 110 091
Phone : 011 2279 5505 Telefax : 011 2279 5641
aakarbooks@gmail.com; www.aakarbooks.com

In association with
THE OTHER MEDIA
C 44, IInd Floor, Housing Society
South Extension Part I, New Delhi 110 049
Phones : 011 2462 9372/73 Fax : 011 4104 2271
Email : tom@theothermedia.org

Printed at
Mudrak, 30 A Patparganj, Delhi 110 091

DISCLAIMER

The author and the editorial collective are solely responsible for the contents of this report. The views expressed in this report do not necessarily reflect the views of institutions who supported the research nor Foundation for Ecological Security who supported printing.

Acknowledgements

The Status Report of Adivasis/Indigenous Peoples (SAIP) has been an important initiative of The Other Media and All India Coordinating Forum of Adivasis/Indigenous Peoples. It began with a lot of interest and enthusiasm with a wide consultation among activists, scholars and researchers interested in the Adivasis/Indigenous People's issues. However, the process seemed to have had its own pace and could not keep up with the expectation of completing the report on time. The present phase of the programme has covered, state-wise, issues of land and mining in the Adivasis/Indigenous People's areas.

This report on land issues in the Adivasi areas of Orissa has been prepared by Kundan Kumar with P R Choudhury, Soumen Sarangi, Pradeep Mishra and Sricharan Behera. We gratefully acknowledge the efforts made by the authors and members of the Editorial Collective (EC) in preparing this report.

Members of the EC went through the reports and gave their valuable comments and suggestions on the report. We gratefully acknowledge their contribution that was available at every stage of preparation of the report. The efforts of the EC have been untiringly coordinated by C R Bijoy. The reports owe a lot to his relentless efforts to keep in the loop everyone concerned towards producing good results out of the reports. At the level of The Other Media, Ravi Hemadri, who worked as the Executive Director of the organisation through most part of the programme served as a link between the organisation and the EC. He continued to coordinate the final editing and printing of the reports. We gratefully acknowledge the role played by both C R Bijoy and Ravi Hemadri.

We acknowledge and thank the Adivasi Academy, Tejgarh, Gujarat, and particularly Prof Ganesh Devy, for generously hosting in February, 2008, a two-day workshop of members of the EC and authors to review the draft reports. We thank the members of the Advisory Board of the SAIP, who with their participation in the first consultation and later whenever called upon, gave their inputs to the reports. Thanks are due to Shankar Gopalakrishnan who meticulously put together statistical data and selected literature for SAIP.

Finally we would like to acknowledge and thank our funders ICCO, Netherlands, and TROCAIRE, Ireland, who supported the programme right through the last five years. We are grateful to the Foundation for Ecological Security, Anand, Gujarat, who generously supported the printing of the first phase of reports on land. We thank all of them for being patient with this initiative.

December, 2010

E Deenadayalan
General Secretary

Contents

Preface

Eighty-eight million Adivasis and indigenous peoples live in India – approximately one fourth of the world's total indigenous population. Historically self-sufficient, forest-based communities with independent cultural identities, they have been subjected to displacement, dispossession and repression for more than a century and are now India's poorest and most marginalised communities. Since the onset of British rule, and in many cases from much earlier, Adivasis and indigenous peoples have been systematically and forcibly dispossessed of the resources of their homelands. In gross violation of democratic practice, social justice and both constitutional and legal requirements, such dispossession continues to this day. It is also the Adivasis and indigenous peoples who have paid the heaviest price for the current neo-liberal globalisation policies, with their land, resources and forests taken from them for private capital - in the name of 'economic growth.'

These larger processes have been accompanied by the erosion and undermining of cultural identities, leading to a loss of cultural moorings and other markers of ethnicity. Less than half of India's Adivasi communities speak their own language. State and private efforts at 'mainstreaming' and against indigenous faiths, practices and cultural mores have had a devastating impact.

Such trends have not gone unchallenged. Despite growing differentiation, ethnicity has emerged as a strong, consolidating force. Many have organised, often with the help of sympathetic outsiders, to fight against their oppressors and struggle for the control over land and other resources, and for local self-government as in parts of Central India. There have been demands for political self-determination and autonomy of varying degrees as in Jharkhand and the north-east. The state characterises all such struggles as 'Law and Order Problems', and large parts of central India and the north-east are heavily militarised in the name of 'national security'. In other parts too state repression has been heavy and brutal.

Though these processes are well known to many and particularly to Adivasis and indigenous people's movements, there continues to be a dearth of knowledge on the overall status of Adivasis and indigenous peoples in India. The struggle-based mass organisations of Adivasis and indigenous peoples in the Indian subcontinent articulated the need to work towards such a task in the late 1990s. The collective process to fulfil this task was launched in 2005.

The Status of Adivasis/Indigenous Peoples is conceptualised as a series of reports on salient themes affecting the lives of Adivasis/Indigenous Peoples. In the first instance, the series focuses on the situation of land and mining in the tribal tracts of the country. We hope that the series will be effective in not only deliberating upon similar themes of importance to the Adivasi present and future, but also help strengthening linkages amongst movements, activists, scholars and all others who are concerned with the protection of the rights of Adivasis/Indigenous Peoples in the Indian subcontinent.

This series of reports will explore the history, the laws, and the facts, and describe struggles while providing an overview of current realities. The main purpose of these reports is to expand linkages and relationships between movements, scholars, and activists so that the future of the political struggles is informed and forward looking.

Executive Summary

Access to land and land-based resources has been a critical issue for the Adivasi communities in forested landscapes of Central India, including Orissa. Though land and land-based resources are central to the livelihoods of Adivasis, they have poor access to land and forests. Poor access to land resources seems to be a major reason underlying chronic poverty among Adivasis and the recurrent conflicts in the region. The loss of private landholdings by Adivasis has been a cause of concern. However, as this paper shows, poor access to land is not only the outcome of land alienation to non-Adivasis, but is also the outcome of land and forest policies followed by the State. The paper identifies some of the main processes which have led to poor access to land for the Adivasis. The major typologies affecting Adivasi access to land have been categorised into loss of land settled with Adivasis through private transactions, lack of proper recording of occupation rights through survey and settlements, classification of land as forest land, displacement through land acquisition under development projects and poor implementation of land regularisation and distribution. The paper discusses these typologies in detail with examples and illustrations. It discusses some of the possible steps which can be taken to ameliorate the current situation.

Introduction[1]

Land and land-based resources are central to the social and cultural existence of Adivasis. The majority of the Adivasis in India reside in mountainous, forested landscapes in North East India and the vast forested upland tracts of Central India. The central Indian Adivasi homeland cover nearly 100 districts in eight states of the country stretching from Banswara (Rajasthan) in the west to Purulia (West Bengal) in the east. These districts together account for about 55 million tribal people (roughly 70% of India's tribal population) spread over 68 million hectares of geographical area.[2]

The British identified alienation of land from Adivasis as an important political and administrative issue leading to unrest and rebellions, and passed special laws to protect Adivasi rights in land. Protection of land rights of tribal

1. The paper is based on a Study "A Socio-Economic and Legal Study of Tribal Land in Orissa" carried out by the author for the World Bank, Washington D.C. The study used intensive study of laws and policies of the Government of Orissa, and also conducted field studies in three districts of Orissa.
2. Phansalkar, S. J. and Verma, S., 2004. Improving Water Control as a Strategy for Enhancing Tribal Livelihoods, *Economic and Political Weekly*. 31 July.

communities was also incorporated into Indian Constitution through Schedule V and VI. Historically, alienation of land from tribals has been recognised as an important political and administrative issue.

Legally, alienation of land is defined as the loss of *patta* or private land – i.e. loss of land on which the cultivator has *rayati* or tenancy rights. This perspective does not factor in the communal ownership system practised by many Adivasi groups traditionally. Except for north-east India, communal or corporate ownership of land was not recognised by the land and forest administration systems introduced by the British or the postcolonial Indian State. Loss of access to land and forests which have been classified as state-owned and diverted for various purposes, have rarely figured in the official discourse of tribal land alienation. However, a review of the literature dealing with poverty and livelihoods among tribal communities clearly brings out that, apart from alienation of private land, diversion of land for different purposes by the state has also played an important role in reducing access to land by tribals. These diversions include diversion of land for development projects, notification of government forests, large-scale plantation programmes etc. Thus, understanding constraints on Adivasi access to land also needs to take into account these processes along with the alienation of land legally owned by Adivasis.

1

Scheduled Tribes in Orissa

'Scheduled Tribes constitute nearly 22.21% of the total population of Orissa. Sixty-two communities have been designated as Scheduled Tribes in the State of which 13 have been recognised as Primitive Tribal Groups. Nearly half the State's area (44.70%) is under Schedule V of the Indian Constitution, with a total population of 8,870,884 (1991 census), out of which 58% are tribals and 20% are Scheduled Castes.[3] The main tribes are Kondhs, Gonds, Santals, Mundas, Oraons, Bhattadas, Bhumij, Saoras, and Parajas. Many of these communities are traditionally dependent on shifting cultivation.

---

3. The following areas are under Schedule V in Orissa: Mayurbhanj, Sundargarh, Koraput, Rayagada, Nabarangpur and Malkangiri districts in whole, Kuchinda tehsil of Sambalpur district, Keonjhar, Telkoi, Champua, Barbil tehsils of Keonjhar district, Khondamal, Balliguda and G Udayagiri tehsils of Khondamal district, R Udaygiri tehsil, Gumma and Rayagada block of Parlekhemundi tehsil in Parlakhemundi sub-division and Suruda tehsil of Ghumsur sub-division in Ganjam district, Thuamul Rampur and Lanjigarh blocks of Kalahandi district and Nilagiri block of Balasore district. The total area of the Scheduled Areas contain almost 70% of the forest areas of Orissa even though they form only 44% of the State area.

2

Poverty of Scheduled Tribes in Orissa

Orissa is one of the poorest states in India, with an estimated 47% of its population living on less than a dollar a day.[4] A regional and social group-wise analysis of poverty in Orissa highlights the fact that the population in Scheduled Areas is comparatively much poorer than the population in non-Scheduled Areas, and that Scheduled Tribes are the poorest groups. In 1999-2000, 73% of the Scheduled Tribes in Orissa were below the poverty line as compared to 55% and 33% respectively for Scheduled Castes and General Castes.[5] The situation in South Orissa is even worse with approximately 87% of the Scheduled Tribes below the poverty lin, and the socio-economic indicators in some pockets are worse than in sub-Saharan Africa.

---

4. Haan and Dubey, 2003. *Extreme Deprivation in Remote Areas in India: Social Exclusion as Explanatory Concept*, Paper presented at the 'International Conference on Staying Poor: Chronic Poverty and Development Policy', Manchester, IDPM, University of Manchester, 7 to 9 April. http://idpm.man.ac.uk/cprc/Conference/ conferencepapers/Dehaan% 20Arjan%20-dubey%2007.03.03.pdf
5. Ibid.

3

Land-use Systems and Land Ownership in Tribal Districts

Most Adivasis tend to follow a clan-based land tenure system which provides customary rights on land, trees, forests etc. Adivasis like Kondhs, Saoras, Parojas, Gadabas, Bondos, Juangs and Bhuiyans traditionally carry out shifting cultivation in the hills and cultivate paddy in the valleys, which are usually terraced by them. Most swiddening tribes broadly cultivated four types of land – valley paddy lands or wetlands, homesteads/backyards, uplands and swidden or shifting cultivation fields (for a more detailed summary of traditional landuse and tenure patterns please see Kumar et al., 2005).

The traditional land use patterns of the Adivasi communities was ignored by the state (both colonial and post colonial period) which settled a large area of customarily claimed lands as state-owned lands. Thus in Scheduled Areas of Orissa, an average of 74% of the land is categorised as state land, of which 48% is forest land and 26% is non-forest land[6]. Three-fourths of all land in these tribal-dominated

6. Non-forest state land was calculated by subtracting the forest land area and the total operational landholdings in the district from the total area of the district. This could therefore be on the higher side and include areas under reservoirs, etc.

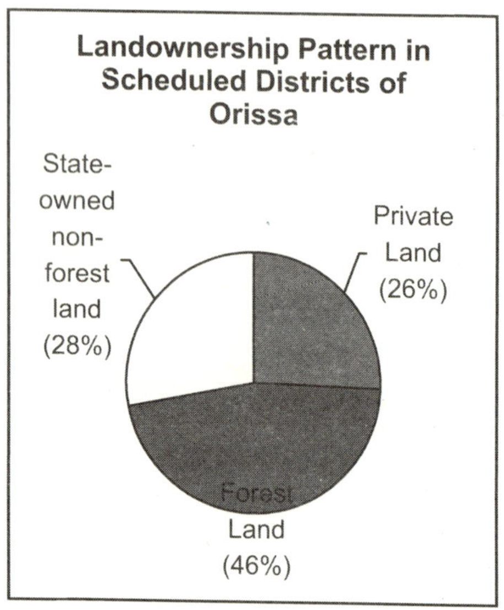

districts belongs to the State, though most of the tribals in these areas are either landless or marginal landowners eking out a predominantly subsistence agriculture-based livelihood. Analysis of secondary data makes the stark problems of tribal access to land in the tribal areas.

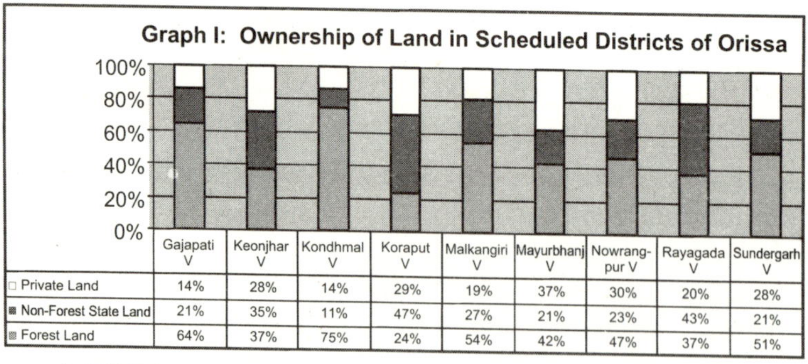

	Gajapati V	Keonjhar V	Kondhmal V	Koraput V	Malkangiri V	Mayurbhanj V	Nowrang-pur V	Rayagada V	Sundergarh V
□ Private Land	14%	28%	14%	29%	19%	37%	30%	20%	28%
■ Non-Forest State Land	21%	35%	11%	47%	27%	21%	23%	43%	21%
▦ Forest Land	64%	37%	75%	24%	54%	42%	47%	37%	51%

A THRTI study taken up in 1978-80 in all tribal sub-plan areas showed that 22.84% of tribal households are landless, whereas 40.46% owned less than 2.5 acres each.[7] Another

7. THRTI, 1987. *The Study of Tribal Land Alienation*, Tribal and Harijan Research and Training Institute, Government of Orissa, Bhubaneswar.

analysis of the Agriculture Census data of 1995-96 in the tribal districts shows that the percentage of tribal landholders having less than one standard acre[8] of land ranges from 41% in Malkangiri to 77% in Gajapati, with average standing at 73% (21% actual landless and 52% legal landless owning 0-1 standard acre).

Gajapati, a tribal-dominated district, has just 14.82% of its total area under cultivators' title, with the rest of the land belonging to the government. Approximately 93% of the rural households in this district have legal title on only 9% of the district's land area. Kondhmal is another tribal district where almost 86% of the land is owned by the State, with 75% of the land categorised as forest lands. In this district, 66% of the rural households own only 7% of the districts land. The situation is even worse in the remote areas inhabited by the Primitive Tribal Groups (PTGs) in Orissa, where almost all the land is owned by the State.

The fact that most of the land in tribal districts is owned by the State reflects in the landholding patterns in these tribal-dominated districts. For instance, the Scheduled Tribe average holdings in Orissa works out to 1.12 standard acres as compared to 1.43 standard acres for general castes[9], even

---

8. The landholdings in standard acres were calculated on the basis of the extent of irrigated and unirrigated holdings. The irrigated holdings were assumed to have two irrigated crops of paddy each year (Class I land- one acre equals one standard acre), whereas unirrigated uplands were assumed to be equivalent to Class IV lands (4.5 acres of Class IV lands is equivalent to one standard acre)
9. When just the landholding is taken without converting it into standard acres, the average landownership of the STs is slightly more than the general caste landowners of the state. However, this does not reflect the fact that much more of the land owned by general castes (concentrated in plain areas of the state)is irrigated as opposed to land owned by ST (concentrated in the hilly tracts of the state). Conversion into standard acres provides a more balanced perspective.

though the general castes mainly stay in plains areas with much lower proportion of state owned land and much higher population density. Scheduled Tribe landowners categorised as marginal landowners comprise 14.8% of the landholdings of Orissa, but they own only 4.8% (in area terms) of all agricultural landholdings, with an average holding of only 0.44 standard acres.

The key to this skewed landownership lies in the fact that rights over communal land and swidden/shifting cultivation were never settled with respective tribal communities. The Forest Enquiry Committee Report of 1959 mentioned that 12,000 sq. miles (almost 30,720 sq. kms.) of land in Orissa were under shifting cultivation[10]. Very little of this vast area was settled with the tribals. These lands were settled either as forest land or as government revenue land. Thus paradoxically, even though three-fourths of the land in tribal districts belongs to the government, most tribals remain landless or marginal landowners. In practice, much of the customary owned land is still under cultivation of the tribals, and is treated by the state as encroached.

The fact that much of the land customarily cultivated by Adivasis has not been settled with them has had major implications for their livelihoods. Combined with ineffectiveness of laws to prevent transfer of tribal *patta* land to non-tribals, this has led to loss of access to land and criminalisation of customary landownership systems. At the same time, the state government has found it very easy to divert customary tribal lands for development and conservation projects as legally, most of this land is government land.

---

10. Government of Orissa, 1959. *Forest Enquiry Report*, Government of Orissa Press, Cuttack.

4

Major Issues Related to Loss of Adivasi Access to Land and Other Natural Resources

There are several processes through which tribals have lost access to land and forests essential for their survival and livelihoods. These include not only alienation of land which is legally owned by the tribals through debt mortgaging and sale, but also loss of access to land through reservation of forests, loss of traditional shifting cultivation land through survey and settlement, displacement, unsuitable and unimplemented land reform laws. Over a period of time, all these processes have led to loss of control and access to livelihood support systems vital to their existence, marginalising and impoverishing tribal communities. The influx of non-tribals over the last two centuries, many of whom are more capable of negotiating state-enforced legal and tenure systems, have pushed Adivasi communities to the bottom of the local power hierarchies, even in areas where they are in the majority. In areas where tribals are in the minority, their living conditions, along with those of Dalits, are even more miserable and powerless. Lack of ownership and claim over land and other factors of production is one of the fundamental reasons behind the current situation.

Historically, land survey and settlements and cash land revenue monetised the economy and led to large-scale indebtedness amongst Adivasi societies. The princely rulers and British rulers also preferred to settle lands with non-Adivasis who carried out settled cultivation rather than shifting cultivation on hills. Slowly, Adivasi intermediary tenure holders were replaced by non-Adivasi tenure holders in many areas. In the Gangpur Princely State, most *gaontias* (intermediary tenure holders responsible for rent collection) were Adivasis in the early 1800s, but by the 1890s there was a greater preference for non-Adivasi *gaontias* from Agharia and Teli castes.[11] Influx of non-Adivasi peasantry into Adivasi areas was actively encouraged and facilitated by the rulers, and opposition of Adivasis to this influx was suppressed by force wherever required. The process of loss of territory by Adivasis was aided by creation of intermediary tenure holders who were mostly non-Adivasis and had effective administrative control of the area under their jurisdiction.

Simultaneously, increasing importance of forest (timber) based revenue led the British rulers as well as the Princely States to reserve or notify more and more areas as forests under various forest laws and rules, imposing restrictions on the Adivasis using these forests. Restrictions on shifting cultivation on areas designated as forests were one of the key strategies for increasing the commercial value of these lands. The takeover of forested lands was based on non-recognition of customary Adivasi land rights over these areas by the state. Clan and lineage territories were not recognised in the forest settlement operations. Often such forest notifications were carried out without proper survey and settlement of even recognised rights of permanent cultivation.

Thus Adivasis faced loss of land on two accounts in the pre-independence era – the lowlands and paddy lands held under private ownership were lost owing to influx of non-Adivasis, non-recognition of rights, indebtedness and

---

11. Pati, B., 1993. *Resisting Domination: Peasants, Tribals, and the National Movement in Orissa, 1920-50*. Manohar Publishers & Distributors, New Delhi,

inability to pay land revenue. The shifting cultivation lands were lost due to notification of this land as forests or government land. Both these processes were aided by the expansion of state and markets into the Adivasi areas. These trends have continued even after independence.

The chart below delineates some of the processes through which Adivasis have lost access to land in Orissa:

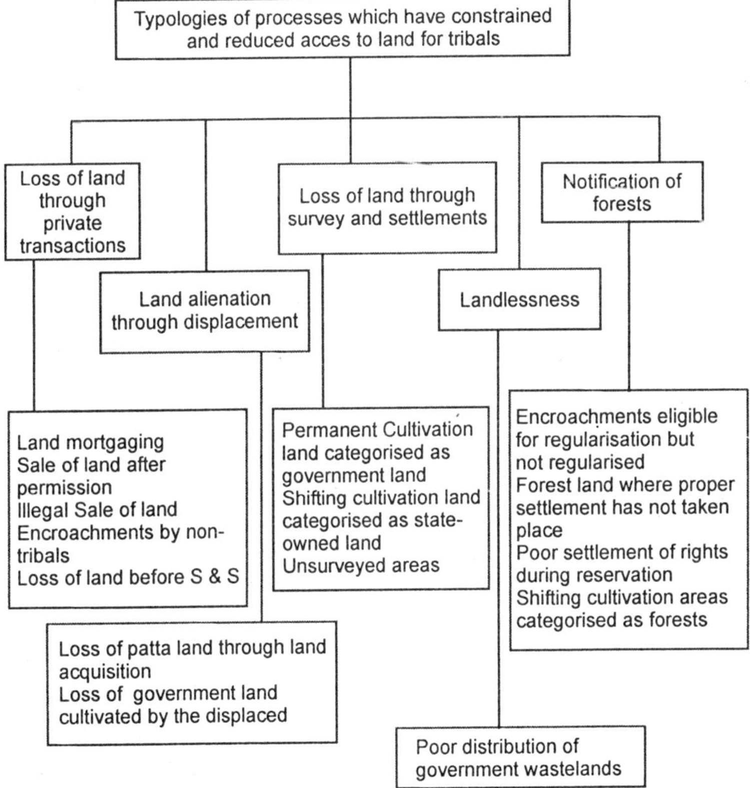

4.1 Loss of Private Land

Three-fourths of the land in the tribal districts belongs to the State Government. Our analysis shows that of the rest (25%) settled with the landholders in these districts, 64% of the land belongs to tribals. The average landholding of tribal households in these tribal districts is only 1.06 standard acres, with approximately 20% of households being landless and 65% being small and marginal farmers. Even this land is being lost by the Scheduled Tribes through different processes, including informal mortgaging and sale of land, legal and illegal.

Transfer[12] of tribal land to non-tribals was forbidden through the Orissa Land Reform (OLR) Act, 1960, for the non-Scheduled Areas and by the Orissa Scheduled Areas Transfer of Immovable Property (by Scheduled Tribes) Regulation 1956 (OSATIP) for the Scheduled Areas, except with the permission of competent authorities. A large number of such permissions were given up to 1995. In 2002, the Orissa Government amended the OSATIP Regulation, banning outright all transfer of tribal-owned land to non-tribals in the Scheduled Areas.

Viegas's study in four districts of Orissa found that Scheduled Tribes had lost almost 56% of their private land, out of which 40% was lost through debts and mortgages and the rest through personal sales.[13] Another study by Dash in 18 villages in Koraput district found that ST families in these villages lost 13.72% of their land during the period 1990-94. Out of these, 51% was lost through sale after permission from district authorities, 26% through mortgage and 15% by oral transfer.[14]

Informal mortgaging of land is one of the most important modes of private land alienation in both our case studies and in secondary literature. The most important reason for mortgaging of land was family ceremonies (marriages and deaths) and health. A four village study with a sample of 483 households found that 49 tribal households had mortgaged

12. Transfer is the relevant laws is defined as
13. Viegas, P., 1991. *Encroached and Enslaved: Alienation of Tribal Lands and its Dynamics.*
14. Dash, S.N., 2001. *A Study of the Problem of Land Alienation in Tribal Areas with Special Reference to the District of Koraput*, Utkal University, Bhubaneswar.

out a total of 44.5 acres of land. Of the 49 households, 17 (35%) needed the money for marriages or for funeral ceremonies and 23% borrowed money for health-related factors.[15]

Approximately 8,550 acres of tribal land have been sold after obtaining permission from the authorities during the period 1957-1997 in Orissa under Section 3(1) of the OSATIP Regulation in Orissa.[16]

Before the OSATIP Regulation and the OLR Act became applicable, different laws for protections of tribal lands were present in different parts of Orissa. Most of these laws were full of loopholes and were of little practical use in reducing land transfers to non-tribals.

For example, from 1927-1950, Goudas and Malis (OBCs) and Dombas (SC) were included among the list of hill tribes as per the Agency Tracts Interest and Land Transfer (ATILT) Act, 1917, in the undivided Koraput district. This meant that they could freely purchase land from tribals like Kondhs, Parajas, Gadaba, Koyas, etc. Much of the transfer of private land from tribals to non-tribals through sales or mortgages took place before or during this period.

4.2 Lack of Proper Recording of Occupation Rights, Especially Communal Lands, During the Survey and Settlement

In many of the tribal areas, the survey and settlement process did not formalise the ownership of the land occupied by the Adivasis for agriculture. Clan and lineage based territories used by Adivasis were not recognised in the settlement processes. The communal nature of ownership of land, especially swidden land, among tribes like Juangs, Kutia Kondhs, etc. was totally ignored, and such areas were

15. Panigrahi. N., 2001. Impact of State Policies on Management of Land Resources in Tribal Areas of Orissa, *Man & Development*, March.
16. Ibid.

classified as government land.[17] Even in tribes where customary individual ownerships over hillsides were recognised, the cultivated hill slopes were settled as government land.

The most important factor in loss of land by Scheduled Tribes has been the non-recognition of rights on shifting cultivation lands. Estimates of the area under shifting cultivation in Orissa range from 5298 sq. kms. to 37,000 sq. kms.[18] The Forest Enquiry Committee Report of 1959 mentioned that 12,000 sq. miles (almost 30,720 sq. kms.) of land in Orissa were under shifting cultivation.[19] All these lands were lost to the tribal communities through survey and settlements and forest reservations.

In undivided Koraput, during the first survey and settlement processes (1938-1964), the Board of Revenue ruled that since shifting cultivators are not in continuous possession of land for 12 years, they cannot be treated as *ryots* according to the Madras Estate Land Act, 1908, and therefore these lands were not to be settled in their name.[20]

---

17. Rath, B., 2005. *Vulnerable Tribal Livelihood and Shifting Cultivation: The Situation in Orissa with a Case Study in the Bhuyan-Juang Pirh of Keonjhar District*, Vasundhara, Bhubaneswar; and Padel, F., 1995. *The Sacrifice of Human Being: British Rule and the Konds of Orissa*, Delhi, Oxford University Press, New York.
18. Pattnaik, N., 1993. *Swidden Cultivation Amongst Two Tribes of Orissa*, CENDERET, Bhubaneswar, SIDA, New Delhi, and ISO/SWEDFOREST, Bhubaneswar; and Thangam, E S., 1984. *Agro-forestry in Shifting Cultivation Control Programmes in India in Social, Economic, and Institutional Aspects of Agroforestry*, Jackson, J.K. and United Nations University Tokyo, Japan.
19. Government of Orissa, 1995 *A Decade of Forestry*, Orissa Forest Department, Government of Orissa, Bhubaneswar.
20. Behuria, N.C., 1965. *Final Report on the Major Settlement Operation in Koraput District, 1938-64*, Board of Revenue, Government of Orissa.

Box 1: Board of Revenue's decision on shifting cultivation in Koraput during survey and settlement (Behuria, 1965)

Regarding the manner of recording the *podu* lands the Board ordered as follows:

- All lands in **continuous cultivating possession for 12 years before vesting of Jeypore Estate in the State Government whether they are situated above or below 10% slopes**, may be recorded as *ryoti* lands in favour of the person in actual cultivating possession of the same.
- All lands which are above or below 10% slopes which are unoccupied will be recorded as government lands.
- All lands on hill slopes **which are not in the continuous possession of 12 years** at the time of vesting of Jeypore Estate in the State Government may be recorded as government lands. But the concerned plot in the remarks column of the Record of Rights it may be noted that so and so is in the forcible possession of the lands from such and such years.

Box 2: Impact of Non-settlement of Shifting Cultivation Areas in Dekapar Village, Koraput District

In Dekapar, terracing on hillsides and shifting cultivation have been practised traditionally. None of the shifting cultivation areas including the terraced areas were settled with the Kandh tribals, and they were categorised as State-owned unculturable wastelands (*Abad Ajogya Anabadi*) in the Record of Rights. Out of approximately 1,100 acres of land within the traditional boundary of Dekapar village, only 152 acres of land have been settled with the cultivators. Approximately 126 acres of area declared as government land are being cultivated as of now, and the villagers claim to have lost access to an additional 142 acres of land owning to plantations taken up under different programmes. Thus, according to the information collected from the villagers, apart from the 152 acres settled with as *patta* land, approximately another 287 acres, almost all of them on higher slopes, was their customary shifting cultivation land. Even this seems like quite an underestimate, as almost the whole of the hillsides next to the settlement have been under cultivation at one time or another and one or the other family lays claim to such lands.

Box 3: Areas left out of survey and settlement in undivided Koraput district

The survey and settlement in Koraput were carried out in 1938-1964. The survey and settlement covered an area of 6740 sq. miles (17,254.40 sq kms.) out of a total area of 25,320.96 sq. kms., and excluded the following areas:

- All Reserved and Protected Land
- Forests proposed for Reservation in 239 villages of Mathili and Malkangiri
- Police station area and 199 villages in Motu, Kalimela, Podia and Padmagiri areas of Malkangiri subdivision (now Malkangiri district)
- Thickly forested tracts in 1,763 villages in Bissamcuttack and Gunupur tehsils (now part of Rayagada district) and Narayanpatna, Pattangi, Padwa, Laxmipur,Gumma, Kakirigumma and Dasamanthpur areas (now part of Koraput district).
- Bonda Hills and Kondakamberu areas covering approximately 446 sq. miles (now Malkangiri district)

(Behuria, 1965)

Thus the survey and settlement left out approximately 8000 sq. kms. of area, part of which has been surveyed later. However, the lands classified as reserved and protected have never undergone rigorous survey and settlement.

Apart from the above, all land above 10% slope line was left unsurveyed without any rights settlement, and was mostly categorised as either uncultivable wastelands or Jungle Blocks. Thus out of the total area of 17,254.40 sq. kms. which was supposed to have been surveyed, 5,289.08 sq. kms. was classified as *Abad Ajogya Anabadi* (uncultivable wastelands), most of which would be the lands located above the 10% slope in the surveyed areas and used for shifting cultivation (Behuria, 1965). The implication of the above figures is that 13,000 sq. kms. of the undivided Koraput district, i.e. almost 50% of the district's area was never surveyed and rights were not settled.

Decisions not to settle shifting cultivation land were also taken in the tribal parts of then Ganjam district (current

Gajapati), Phulbani District (now Kandhamal district), Juangpirh and Bhuyanpirh of Keonjhar district. The vast shifting cultivation areas passed to the exclusive ownership of the Revenue Department or Forest Department. These decisions have had a far-reaching impact on tribal economy and welfare by denying them rights over land that they had cultivated for generations.

According to per government sources, approximately 640,702 acres of land in Orissa have not been covered under the survey and settlement process at all. Most of these are remote hilly areas inhabited by tribals, including primitive tribes. However, this also seems to be an underestimate. For instance, the surveys and settlements in undivided Koraput district left out vast stretches of land including all Reserved Land and Protected Land. The survey and settlement of land was limited to below the 10% slope line. Box no 3 shows the areas in Koraput which were left unsurveyed (and unsettled) during the survey and settlement, 1938-1964. It seems that almost half the total area of the undivided Koraput district was not surveyed and settled.

In the absence of settlement of rights in these areas, effectively rights were denied. This is especially true of land categorised as forests which have not been surveyed, including the vast areas categorised as deemed reserved or protected forests. Similarly, the areas above 10% slope have been simply categorised as government land of various categories without settling the rights of tribal cultivators.

In revisional settlements, permanent cultivation by tribals on land categorised as government land was often not regularised in their names, even though they were eligible for settlement. The tribals allege that settlement officers ask for bribes for settling such lands in their names. The Vedanta case below (Box 4) illustrates the situation.

Box 4: Eviction of landless Adivasis from land acquired for Vedanta Alumina Ltd., Lanjigarh Block, Kalahandi district

Almost 64 landless Kondh households (Scheduled Tribes) of the Jaganathpur Village had been cultivating Khata no. 186, categorised as revenue land, for the last 30-40 years. Encroachment cases for the cultivation had been filed by the Revenue Department against many of these people. The encroachment notices show that these Scheduled Tribes have been in physical possession of these lands for at least last seven to eight years. However, the tribals claim that even their forefathers were cultivating the land. Both as per the principle of adverse possession and as per the Section 7(a) of Orissa Prevention of Land Encroachment Act 1972, such land should have been settled with the landless persons to the extent of one standard acre (equivalent to 4.5 acres of uplands). The last revisional survey and settlement of Lanjigarh block took place in the late 1980s, and the tribals claim that when they tried to get the land regularised in their names, they were asked to pay bribes up to Rs. 5,000/- per acre, which they could not afford. Even after the settlement, they have been trying to get the land regularised through Revenue Department, but have been asked for bribes by the Revenue Department personnel.

In 2003, instead of settling this land with the tribal cultivators cultivating these lands, the district administration summarily evicted these 64 families by force without any compensation, thereby taking away their main source of livelihood. The land has been handed over by the district administration to Vedanta Alumina Ltd. for the construction of their rehabilitation colony. In law, this action violates not only the rule of adverse possession and Section 7(a) of OPLE 1972; it also violates the protection provided to the Scheduled Tribes in Schedule V of the Constitution and Section 3(iii) of the OSATIP Regulation by turning Scheduled Tribes 'effectively' landless. Section 3(iii) of OSATIP regulation (1956) provides a minimum benchmark of 2 acres of irrigated or five acres of unirrigated land for ownership by Scheduled Tribes before any land in their possession can be transferred. By not recognising their cultivation rights and by evicting landless Scheduled Tribe persons from the land cultivated by them for generations, the provision is violated.

Non-settlement of government land cultivated by them is one of the most common complaints by tribals. Regularisation of encroachments invariably requires speed money, and those who can't pay, don't get their land regularised either during the settlements or through the revenue administration.

4.3 Forests and Forest Lands

Forty-six per cent of the land in tribal districts is categorised as forests. Declaration of customary Adivasi lands as forest has been an important factor in loss of Adivasi land. According to official data, Orissa has 58,135 sq. kms. of its area recorded as forest. Only 48,838 sq. kms. of forest land has forest cover of 10% or more.[21] Thus almost 10,000 sq. kms. has a crown cover of less than 10%, i.e. either they are scrub forests or have no forests at all.

The main legislations affecting forest land are the Forest Conservation Act, 1980, and the Orissa Forest Act, 1972 (which repealed the Madras Forest Act in ex-Madras Presidency areas and the Indian Forest Act in the rest of Orissa). The Orissa Forest Act defines two categories of forests: Reserved Forest and Protected Forests. Reserved Forests can be notified as such under Section 21 of the OFA only after settlement of rights as per Section 4-20 of the OFA. As per Section 33 of the Orissa Forest Act, the State Government can also declare any land which is the property of the Government to be Protected Forest only 'if the nature and extents of rights of government and of private persons and village communities in or over the land comprised therein has been inquired into and recorded at a survey and settlement or in such other manner as may be prescribed.'

Thus, prima facie, the forest laws provide protection for settlement of rights of the local people and communities before declaration of forest land. However, this presumption often does not hold true on the ground because of a number of factors. These include:

21. *Forest Survey of India*, 1999.

- Declaration of *deemed* Reserved Forests and Protected Forests
- Non-recognition of rights on land used for shifting cultivation
- Lack of settlement of rights and faulty settlement of rights

4.3.1 Declaration of Deemed Reserved Forests and Protected Forests

Pre-independence, almost all Princely States in Orissa had their own Forest Acts or Rules, based on the Indian Forest Act 1927 or the Madras Forest Act 1885. The Princely States, as per the provisions of these acts or rules, declared certain forested areas as reserved forests or as other classifications of forests. In most cases, proper survey and settlements of rights as prescribed in the IFA 1927 or the Madras Forest Act 1885 were not followed and government forests were declared in an ad hoc fashion. Ramdhyani, in his inquiry of the princely states during the 1940s, pointed out that 'Reservation of forests has so far been made with little consideration for the interests of cultivators and probably by summary orders'.[22] Often the areas declared as forests had existing settlements, especially in those tribal areas where no detailed revenue survey and settlement had taken place. For example, in the year 1943, the Maharaja of Kalahandi had converted 14 whole revenue villages, along with a belt of surrounding reserved forests, as the Leliguma reserved forest, without settling the rights of the villagers.[23]

Post-independence, the Government of Orissa was faced with the problem of status of the forest areas transferred from

---

22. Ramdhyani, R.K., 1947. *Report on Land Tenures and Revenue Systems or Orissa and Chhattisgarh State.*
23. Sundarajan, S., 1963. *Final Report on the Survey and Settlement of the Kashipur, Karlapat, Mahulpatna and Madanpur-Rampur Ex-Zemindaries in the District of Kalahandi,* Orissa Government Press, Cuttack.

the ex-princely states. This was resolved by amending the IFA 1927 in 1954. The amendment through Section 20-A (1) provided that all areas which were reserved forests in the princely states would automatically be deemed to be reserved forests under the IFA 1927. Through the amendment, the newly introduced Section 20-A(4) of the IFA 1927 also laid down that *forests recognised in the merged territories as Khesara Forest, village forest or protected forests or forests by any other name designated or locally known, shall be deemed to be protected forests within the meaning of this Act*. Thus all the 'Reserved Forests' and other forests in merged ex-state areas were converted into Reserved Forests or Protected Forests as defined under the IFA 1927, even though most of these areas had not been properly surveyed and rights settled as required by the law.

In princely states like Bamra (present-day Deogarh district and Kuchinda tehsil of Sambalpur district), Athamalik, Pallahara (presently part of Angul district), Boudh (Boudh district), Bonai (currently part of Sundargarh district), Daspalla (currently part of Nayagarh district) and Rairakhol (currently part of Sambalpur district), all wastelands not declared as reserved forests or protected forests were declared to be *Khesara*[24] forests, whether they had forests or not. These were in turn automatically converted

24. Khesara forests were essentially land which was considered as forest, without the stringent provisions of reservation. There were provisions in the forest rules of the princely states to regulate the use of these lands. However, their conversion into agriculture by tenants was actively encouraged to increase land revenue. In the Revenue survey and settlements carried out before 1980 (before FCA, 1980), in general areas under Khesara forests taken up for cultivation would be settled in the name of the cultivators. However, in many areas, no proper Revenue survey and settlement was taken up, or the survey and settlement was taken up after 1980, and as the *Khesara* forests were included in the category of forest land as per FCA 1980, these lands were not settled with the cultivators.

into deemed protected forests as a result of the amendment to the IFA.

Similarly, in the erstwhile Agency Tracts of Madras Presidency, i.e. the undivided Koraput district and Gajapati districts, Reserved and Protected Lands declared under Chapter III of the Madras Forest Act 1882, were deemed to be Protected Forests under the Orissa Forest Act 1972 (Section 33(4)). These forest areas were neither surveyed nor the rights of the cultivators and inhabitants settled at any time.

Thus, in almost all the above forests which are treated as deemed forests, Reserved or Protected, no proper settlement of rights of the inhabitants have been carried out either through the forest settlement process under forest laws or through the survey and settlement processes under the Revenue laws. Large numbers of people, especially tribals, have lived in these forests for generations but are now considered to be encroachers. After the passing of the Forest Conservation Act, 1980, such areas could not be converted to non-forest categories without permission from Ministry of Environment and Forest, Government of India, and hence are frozen as forest land.

4.3.2 Poor Settlement of Rights during Forest Reservation and Demarcation

Even where the forest settlement process was followed as per the forest laws, proper rights settlement has not been carried out. Much of the area that were used as forest fallows for shifting cultivation by the Adivasi communities have been declared as reserved forests, thereby disallowing any access to these lands for cultivation. The renowned anthropologist Verrier Elwin pointed out that in the 1930s-40s, Kondh villagers were approached by forest guards who had orders to demarcate 'reserved forests'; in almost every case the forest guards demanded bribes, and if the villagers refused to pay, he designated the Kondhs' forest fallows as reserved forests.[25]

25. Padel, op. cit.

Even where reserved forests and protected forests have been declared after independence, the forest settlement processes were often not properly implemented. This has happened where forest areas had been left out of revenue settlement processes and therefore the rights of the inhabitants were not formalised. For example, some of the reserved forests in Kondhmal district were declared in the 1960s, before any comprehensive revenue survey and settlement had taken place. These reservations were arbitrary and done primarily on paper, and remote Adivasi settlements inside the forests were included within reserved forests. For instance, Baghnadi RF in the Phiringia Range of Phulbani Division was declared to be a reserved forest in 1968, much before any rights were recognised as per the revenue survey and settlement; local villagers say that there was neither any survey, nor were they informed about the formation of the RF. Almost twenty tribal settlements were included inside the reserved forest. It was only in 1986 that the areas of these villages were dereserved and recategorised as revenue land. However, it seems that in other areas, the tribal settlements inside such reserved forests continue to be treated as encroachments.

4.3.3 Lack of Effort for Regularisation of Eligible Cultivation on Forest Land

Given the magnitude of the problem of cultivation on land categorised as forests, there was a decision by the Orissa Government in 1972 to settle the rights of cultivators on forest land. The state government passed a resolution[26] to release such cultivated areas for settlement of rights in favour of tribals and other backward groups and landless[27]. An order was issued for constituting sub-divisional committees for

26. Resolution no. 32823GE (GL)- 69/72-R dated June 10, 1972 of the State Government of Orissa
27. A household with less than one standard acres of land is treated as landless according to OPLE 1972.

conducting comprehensive surveys of all forest lands to identify areas which would be set apart for agricultural use.

However the identification and regularisation in name of cultivators could not be completed before 1980, when the Forest Conservation Act (FCA) was passed. The statistics concerning 11 districts (out of a total of 13 at the time) show that a total area of 0.276 million acres of forestland was under cultivation. The FCA effectively led to the freezing of the process of regularisation of cultivation on forest lands. This left large patches of permanent cultivation in forest area unregularised, and now these areas are being treated as encroachments.

In 1990, the Ministry of Environment and Forests (MoEF) of the Central Government issued an order which provided guidelines on regularisation of eligible forest encroachments. Based on these guidelines, a circular of the Government of Orissa, along with the guidelines, were sent to all collectors asking for regularisation of eligible forest lands encroached before 1980. Nothing seems to have happened at the ground level despite repeated reminders. After the 1996 order of the Supreme Court in the *Godavarman* case, a meeting of the Tribal Advisory Council in January 1997 under the chairmanship of the Chief Minister, took the decision to expedite the process of land settlement as per the 1990 MoEF guidelines. In 2000, the Orissa government submitted a proposal to the MoEF for regularising 4,429 ha. of forest area for cultivation. The figure of 4,429 ha. is a gross underestimate[28] of the ground situation (Table 5). This proposal was cleared by the Supreme Court in 2007 but the

28. Apparently the main basis of accepting whether any cultivation on forest land was pre-1980 and therefore eligible for regularisation was whether a case of encroachment has been filed against the cultivator before 1980. Unfortunately, in most cases of cultivation on forest land, no cases had been filed, and these were rendered.

effective regularisation on the ground hasn't been carried out.[29]

Along with the 1990 circular on regularisation of forest land "encroachments," the MoEF issued another circular which pertained to the review of disputed claims over forest land arising out of incomplete or flawed forest settlement processes. The circular deals with situations wherein rights of inhabitants on forest land were not enquired into and settled as per law before the land was notified as forests. The circular provides for the review of disputed claims arising from

- 'deemed reserved forests'
- Claims in tribal areas where there is prima facie evidence that forest settlement was not proper because of incorrect maps/records or because the affected persons were not provided information properly.
- Claims in tribal areas where the forest settlement is over but the final notification under Section 20 of the IFA 1927 is yet to be made.

The circular asked the State Government to constitute committees, examine the above cases, and submit proposals to the MoEF for providing titles to genuinely affected persons. In spite of the fact that most of the reserved forests in Orissa are deemed reserved forests, and that there are large areas of forests where settlements have been done, but the final notification under Section 21 of OFA 1972 (equivalent to Section 20 of IFA 1927) has not been done, there has been no effort from the State Government to submit claims with respect to these areas.

The issue of tribal rights on forest land was included in the Common Minimum Programme of the UPA government

---

29. The Supreme Court has given orders dated November 13, 2000 restraining de-reservation of forests till further orders and another order dated November 23, 2001 restraining regularisation of encroachment on forest land till further orders.

at the Centre, and the Scheduled Tribes and Other Traditional Forest Dwellers (Recognition of Forest Rights) Act was enacted in 2006. However, the bureaucracy, particularly the forest bureaucracy and the conservationists are opposing its implementation.

4.4 Poor Implementation of Land Regularisation and Distribution as per OLR Act 1960, OGLS Act 1962 and OPLE Act 1972

The laws and policies dealing with land and forest rights settlement have many weaknesses which have manifested themselves in insecure rights of Adivasis over their land and natural resources. At the same time, proper implementation of other existing laws which could have helped ameliorate the situation has also been lacking greatly. Such laws include the Orissa Land Reforms Act, 1960, the Orissa Government Land Settlement Act, 1962, and the Orissa Prevention of Land Encroachment Act, 1972.

The provisions of the OGLS Act say that SCs and STs should be provided land to the extent of 70% of the state-owned land eligible for settlement in a village. This does not seem to have been followed properly. Similarly, the provision of OPLE 1972 [Section 7(2a)], regarding regularisation of encroachment up to one standard acre seems to have been honoured in the breach. This is despite the fact that almost 50% of the Scheduled Tribe cultivators are marginal and landless in the Scheduled Areas, with an average landholding of 0.45 standard acres only.[30] According to the State Government, there are 150,000 landless tribal families in the State, with 14,913 families in Mayurbhanj, followed by Rayagada (14,120 families) and Koraput (11672 families).

The State Government distributed 377,000 acres of land to 224,000 Scheduled Tribe families since 1974-75. However, most of the land distribution took place in the late 1970s. In

30. This data is based on calculations carried out on the basis of the Agricultural Census, 1995-96.

the decade of 1980-1990, a total of 23,540 acres were distributed to 16,580 ST families. In 1988-89 to 1998-99, 13,804 acres of land was distributed to 12,752 families. In the last five years, 11,173 acres of land were distributed to 10,540 families. At the current rate of land distribution, distributing land to 150,000 landless families will take at least seventy years.

There is a clear need to accelerate the land distribution programme to tribal households, especially in districts where sufficient revenue land is available. This include districts like Gajapati, Rayagada, Koraput, parts of Kalahandi (Thuamulrampur and Lanjigarh blocks), Kondhmal, Malkangiri, the Scheduled Areas in Keonjhar, etc.

The number of landless tribal families as provided by the State Government seems to be an underestimate when compared to data from the Agricultural Census, 1995-96. A very preliminary analysis shows that out of 1.7 million operational landholdings held by Scheduled Tribes, approximately 0.58 million landholders are marginal and small farmers with an average holding of 0.44 standard acres. Calculations based on the number of operational landholdings and the census data also show that the number of total rural tribal households (based on the 1991 census data) is approximately 0.3 million households more than the number of operational holdings in 1995-96. The key question is whether this figure of 0.3 million households reflects the actual number of landless Scheduled Tribe households or not. There is a need to identify the landless and the marginal ST households through surveys and study of land records and prioritise distribution of surplus land to such families. At the same time, Bhoodan land and ceiling surplus land lying with the Revenue Department should be distributed expeditiously to landless SC and STs.

In the field studies, many discrepancies have also been observed in cases of land distribution to landless families. While in many cases, the households have not been shown the patches that are distributed to them, in many others they have not been given title documents (*pattas*). There have also been conflicts resulting out of contested ownership between the customary owner and new-legal owner of such lands. In many cases of ceiling surplus distribution, effectively the lands are still being tilled by the old landlords, and the new owners are not allowed possession.

4.5 Displacement through Irrigation, Mining, Industrial and Conservation Projects in Tribal Areas

Orissa is extremely rich in minerals, most of which lie in the tribal districts. The hilly terrain and availability of water in tribal areas also make them suitable for reservoirs and dams . The major dams taken up in Scheduled Areas include the Machkund, Salandi, Balimela, Upper Kolab, Indrawati, and the Mandira Dams. The major industrial projects taken up in Scheduled Areas include the Rourkela steel plant, NALCO's alumina refinery at Damanjodi, and Hindustan Aeronautics Ltd.'s factory at Sunabeda. Several new industrial projects are under implementation or proposed in Scheduled Areas, including the alumina refineries of UAIL in Kashipur and Vedanta at Lanjigarh.

The richness of forests and wildlife has also led to an increasing number of protected areas (wildlife sanctuaries and national parks) in the Scheduled Areas. Such protected areas have created a major problem as the rights of all inhabitants in and around these areas are being extinguished, affecting their livelihoods and sometimes leading to displacement.

Development projects are estimated to have displaced 1.5 million people between 1951 and 1995, of whom 42% were tribals. According to this estimate, less than 25% of the displaced tribals were ever resettled, even partially. Irrigation and hydroelectric projects have been the most important reason of displacement in Scheduled Areas. Except for a few irrigation projects, development projects have not provided land as compensation. Even where the principle of land for land compensation was accepted, often cash compensation was given as suitable land was not available. A study of seven development projects with a sample of 301 households (with 43.8% tribal households within the sample) showed that legal landlessness increased from 15.6% of the households to 58.8% after displacement.[31] More important, since large areas of land cultivated by Scheduled Tribes are not legally settled in their names, they receive no compensation when such land is taken up for development projects. Ota, in his study of displacement in the upper Indravati Project[32], found that on an average, each displaced family had been cultivating 1.50 acres of state-owned and 2.34 acres of private land before displacement, and that 49% of the sampled families were landless. After displacement, landlessness increased to 85.25%, the average legal landholding declined to 0.62 acres and the average government land cultivated came down to only 0.2 acres.[33]

Another important cause of displacement in Schedule V areas is large-scale mining and industrial projects. The most important mining zones within Scheduled Areas are iron ore and manganese mining in Sundargarh and Keonjhar districts and bauxite in Kalahandi, Koraput and Rayagada districts. Apart from displacement, mining and industries also lead to large-scale influx of non-tribals, which often leads to social and political marginalisation of the tribals. The environmental impacts are drastic and affect a much larger number of people than those directly displaced.

Given the liberalisation of mining and industrial policies which allows for direct foreign investments, many mining

---

31. Pandey, B., 1998. *Depriving the Underprivileged for Development*, first edn. Institute for Socio-Economic Development, Bhubaneswar.
32. Ota took a sample of 500 affected families. Of this 42% are tribal households.
33. Ota, Akhil B. 2001. *Reconstructing Livelihood of the Displaced Families in Development Projects: Causes of Failure and Room for Reconstruction*, Anthrobase. Available online at: http://www.anthrobase.com/txt/O/Ota_A_02.htm

and industrial projects are in the pipeline, mostly to be located in Scheduled Areas. Some of these propose to carry out mining in areas inhabited by Primitive Tribal Groups, such as the Dongaria Kondhs in Lanjigarh, Kalahandi and Juangs

Box 5: Compensatory afforestation in Kadalibadi, Juangpirh, Keonjhar

In Kadalibadi, a Juang village in Keonjhar, compensatory afforestation has led to displacement of Juang tribals, a PTG, from their customary swidden land (which is not recorded in their names). In this village, only 25 hectares out of a total area of 283 hectares in the village is legally available to the village residents. 37 out of 44 families hold this 25 hectares, with an average holding size of only 0.66 ha.

During 1993-1999, 77.186 hectares (27% of the village area) was leased to the Forest Department to carry out plantations. This area of 77.186 ha has been diverted from the "uncultivable wasteland" of the village, which is under the control of Revenue Department. Plantations have already been carried out in these lands. In 2005, another 43 ha. (12% of village area) in the village was leased out to the Forest Department for compensatory afforestation. Compensatory afforestation is taken up under the the Forest Conservation Act 1980 in case of diversion of forest land to non-forest use such as mining, reservoirs, etc.

The series of plantations on their customary lands have been a double tragedy for the hapless Juangs. Even though they did not get legal rights on their communal land, they continued to communally cultivate these lands. Conversion of the major part of their communal lands into plantations by the Forest Department has deprived them of the access to these swidden lands and has pushed them to starvation levels. The tragedy has been aggravated because the patch selected for the plantation in 2005 is the largest and the most important shifting cultivation patch. The Juangs were also planning to create permanent paddy land in a part of this patch through diverting a local stream. With compensatory afforestation, this land has effectively become forest land, closing all possibilities of the Juangs ever being able to reclaim it. No swidden paddy cultivation has been taken up this year by the Juangs, and starvation looms in their faces.

and Paudi Bhuiyans in Keonjhar and Sundergarh districts.

Almost all the iron ore mines and deposits are located in the Scheduled Areas of Keonjhar and Sundargarh districts. The situation in these Scheduled Areas are already extremely disturbing, with large scale mining leading to displacement of tribals, destruction of their livelihood support system including forests and water sources, large-scale air and water pollution, and influx of outsiders. This is at the current level of mining. However, the amount of mining in this area is proposed to be increased multifold after the signing of over 40 MoUs for steel plants, most of which will source their iron ore from deposits in the scheduled areas. The effect of such proposed mining, almost all in Scheduled Areas of Keonjhar and Sundergarh, on the local tribal inhabitants, their habitats and their livelihoods can only be imagined.

The major bauxite deposits are also located in Scheduled Areas in Kalahandi, Rayagada and Koraput districts with the major mining being done by NALCO on Panchapatamali of Koraput district. These have been a major source of controversy, with the local tribals opposing proposed mining projects tooth and nail, and the State Government using all possible strategies, including coercion and repression, to make these deposits available to mining multinationals. The resistance of Kashipur tribals against UAIL's mining project and alumina refinery has been going on for over 10 years now. Similarily, flashpoints are building up near proposed bauxite mining in Niyamgiri by Vedanta, Sunger by L&T, Kodingamali by Aditya Aluminium and Maliparbat by Hindalco. The bauxite deposits are all located on top of the highest mountains in South Orissa which are called *Malis*, and are sacred to tribals as they are the source of many perennial streams. These streams are vital to local tribals as they are often the only source of water for drinking and irrigation of fields in summer, and sustain the local agricultural economy. This has created massive resistance against bauxite mining amongst tribals.

In Kashipur, the local tribals have been resisting the bauxite mining and alumina refinery project of Utkal

Alumina India Ltd (UAIL) and till date have not allowed the project to come up, even though the administration has tried its best to push the project through, using both coercion and money. In 2000, matters came to a head when three tribal protestors were shot dead by the police. Similarly in Lanjigarh, there have been strong protests by the local tribals against the establishment of an alumina refinery and proposed mining of Niyamgiri Hills for bauxite. In spite of continuous repression by the administration, the tribals are continuing to resist these projects. A similar situation is now emerging in all tribal areas where industrial projects are being planned. The police firing and killing of twelve tribals in Kalinganagar epitomises the grave dissatisfaction over displacement in all tribal areas. Part of the reason for the strong resistance is the bitter experience of the tribals of Koraput and Rayagada with the earlier projects such as Upper Kolab, Indrawati, HAL, NALCO, etc. which has led to destitution of several tribals and destruction of their livelihood base and their culture. Another important reason is that in spite of most of the land in the area proposed to be acquired being categorised as government land, most of it is under cultivation by the tribals. Thus, in Lanjigarh, while acquiring land for Vedanta, the local tribals cultivating government land were simply evicted without any compensation, destroying their livelihoods.

Conservation programmes including plantations and protected areas have emerged as another major problem related to tribal land in Scheduled V areas. Plantations have been the preferred tactic of the Forest Department and Revenue Department to evict cultivators from shifting cultivation land since the 1960s, leading to continuous conflicts with tribals. The trend continues even now. For example, in the last five years, the Forest Department has taken up 52,800 hectares of plantations in the undivided Koraput district alone. Much of this plantation is taken up on land already being cultivated or under shifting cultivation by tribals. The lack of legal title of tribals on most of the land cultivated by them aggravates this situation. An example of the processes involved and resultant injustices on tribals is given in Box 5. Similar situations are found in many other tribal villages where plantations have been carried out.

Constitution of protected areas under the Wildlife Protection Act 1972 (WPA 1972) has become another major land-related issue in the Scheduled Areas. Almost 8,111.55 sq. kms. (5%) of Orissa have been declared as protected areas (sanctuaries and national parks). Most of these protected areas are in Scheduled Areas or in areas where the tribal population is high. The Wildlife Protection Act 1972 is a strong regulatory statute which restricts almost all activities inside protected areas. These include restrictions on entry to the sanctuary (Section 27), removal of forest products including NTFPs (except for bona fide self-consumption), regulation or prohibition of grazing or movement of livestock, etc. This effectively exiles people living inside the protected area from civilisation, with restrictions on movement of goods and services.

More than 700 villages are still inside the existing sanctuaries. Apart from these, a large number of unsurveyed villages and settlements exist inside these sanctuaries, mostly of tribal communities, which are treated as encroachments. For example, in the Sunabeda Sanctuary of Nuapada district, there are 30 revenue villages and 34 unsurveyed settlements, mostly inhabited by the Chuktia Bhunjias, a primitive tribal group. According to the Forest Department, these 34 settlements are encroachments in the forest, even though this area is the ancestral homeland of the tribals. In Kotagarh sanctuary of Kandhmal district, there are many unsurveyed tribal villages whose rights have not been settled. The same situation exists inside Lakhari Sanctuary in South Orissa. As per the Wild Life Act, such villages are supposed to be relocated out of the sanctuary areas or evicted, in case they are categorised as "encroachments". Collection of NTFPs and other forest products are totally restricted, making livelihoods extremely difficult. This has been a cause of regular conflict and has led to impoverishment of people living inside these areas.

5

Summing Up the Issues of Tribal Land Access

The above discussion of typologies brings out the complex matrix of policies, laws and local contexts which frames the issue of tribal access to land. In policy circles, land issues have been seen through the simple lens of alienation of tribal land, which provides only a partial picture. It is obvious that the issue of alienation of *patta* land by non-tribals through land mortgages and sale is extremely serious. Historically, this has been the most critical mode of loss of good quality agricultural land by tribals. However, given that there is a strict law which forbids it since 2002 and which allows for restoration of land which has been illegally transferred since 1956, the major intervention in this regard would be to ensure better implementation of this law and extension of similar provisions to non-Scheduled Areas.

The flaws in the survey and settlements, revenue administration and forest declaration which have led to non-recognition of customary tribal land ownership has not been recognised as having an important impact on tribal livelihoods and well-being. However, these have meant that cultivation by tribal on customary lands has become criminalised. Often such lands are diverted by the government for plantations or other activities. In our case studies, we found that tribal households as a result of loss of access to such land occupied by them by government plantations have resorted to migration in Dekapar. Even where tribals continue to cultivate such lands, uncertainty of tenure means that they refrain from investing in these lands nor can they access formal credit for its development, thus catalysing the process of land degradation.

Lack of secure rights over their customary landscapes has meant that the state has been at liberty to displace tribals from their livelihoods and resources easily, without paying any compensation. Hundreds of thousands of tribals have been uprooted in this manner by dams, industries and other development projects, as well as wildlife sanctuaries. Displacement has a devastating impact on the tribal psyche, given their cultural attachment to their land and their clans, and their inability to adjust to new locations. The rehabilitation and resettlement packages have been dismal, even not providing land for land in most situations, leaving the vulnerable tribals to their own devices.

From all matrixes, the situation of tribals in Orissa remains dismal. The current situation continues to exist for many reasons. The tribal communities are held in contempt by the dominant caste-based Hindu society, which holds the reins of power in the State. Evolutionism and negative stereotypes about tribals from the colonial era have merged with the Indian elite's ideas of 'assimilationism' to produce a disdain for tribal culture that is almost universal among the non-tribals who live near Adivasis and have power over them.[34] This contempt and disdain is reflected in the prevalent discourses of 'shifting cultivation' being a 'pernicious and evil' practice, tribals being socially and culturally backward. Any discussion with local officials or local non-tribal elite will bring out these biases – that tribals are dirty, superstitious, ignorant, backward, addicted to drinking, with loose morals, etc. At best, they are 'simple, innocent, straightforward

---

34. Padel, op. cit.

people' who need to be protected and whose culture needs to be preserved.

At the same time, a normality of extortion and exploitation[35] has been established, with lower level policemen, forest guards and revenue officers demanding bribes and benefits from tribals in a routine way. The lack of rights on land and the dependence on forests for livelihoods play into the hands of these petty officials, who extract bribes for each and every 'criminalised' activity necessary for tribals' survival. Thus lack of rights over land and other resources not only leads to extraction of rent from tribals, it also dis-empowers them vis-à-vis the local officials and non-tribals who are much more familiar and conversant with the laws and procedures of bureaucracy.

Even when the culture of tribals is admitted to be special, it is sought to be captured in museums and monographs as show pieces. Padel goes to the extent of calling the present situation in tribal India 'internal colonialism'.[36] The Vedanta and the Kadalibadi cases illustrate the contempt and ease with which tribals are displaced from their customary land. The same processes have been repeated several times in all tribal areas where development projects have been implemented.

Such exploitation and dispossession explains the growing disenchantment of tribal communities with current governance processes, as it fails to address these critical issues. Improving tribal access to land and other natural resources is not even a part of the development discourse in tribal areas, even though hundreds of millions of rupees are being spent on tribal development programmes. Even watershed development programmes, which explicitly focus on development of natural resources and land on a watershed basis, have nowhere addressed these issues. This raises

---

35. Ibid.
36. Ibid.

doubts about the very relevance of these development programmes to the tribal situation.

The situation in Scheduled Areas continues to deteriorate, with increasing conflicts, ingress of non-tribals, increasing mining and industrialisation. The Scheduled Areas of Orissa are part of the forested heartlands of India, where incredible poverty and dispossession exists in tandem, exposing in a glaring fashion the historical injustice committed against these communities. These peaceful verdant landscapes are also fast transforming to a hotbed of violence and conflicts out of the discontent of continued dispossession.

6

What Needs to be Done?

It is difficult to list the changes and reforms required for bringing about an improvement in the current situation, and even more difficult to imagine political will to carry out such changes. Some basic principles which can be followed to deal with the crises of land rights facing tribal communities could be adoption of community ownership concept over land lying within the traditional village/habitation boundaries, acceptance of shifting cultivation as a legitimate agricultural land-use, compliance with the *Samata* judgment relating to non-diversion of tribal land to non-tribals, and so on. Effective land administration and land distribution/provision of rights should be accepted as the core development strategy in tribal areas. Some of these are listed below.

6.1 Comprehensive Survey and Settlements for Tribal Land Rights

Comprehensive revenue survey and settlements in the tribal areas need to be carried out. Such survey and settlements should include provision for settlement of rights on the hill slopes in the name of shifting cultivators, removal of limits on the degree of slopes that can be settled with cultivators, communal rights on land not settled with individuai households within the traditional boundary of the villages, etc.

6.2 Protection and Restoration of Private Land

The laws for regulating transfer of tribal (private) land need to be implemented properly and the strong protection of Orissa Scheduled Areas Transfer of Immovable Property (by Scheduled Tribes) Regulation 1956 should be extended to tribals living outside the Scheduled Areas.

Section 3(b) of the OSATIP Regulation makes it mandatory for any person who is in possession (as on September 4, 2002) of agricultural land, that had at any point between 1956 and 2002 belonged to a Scheduled Tribe person, to submit to the Sub-Collector the details of how he or she came to be in possession of such land. In case the person fails to do so, it is to be presumed that the land has been transferred illegally and the land will be reverted to the original tribal owner. The deadline for the submission of the details was September 2004, which apparently seems to have been further extended. The State Government should take this deadline seriously and strictly deal with those people who illegally possess land after the deadline.

In locations where tribal landlessness is very high and there are no other sources of land, the government could consider purchasing or acquiring land from non-tribals for allocation to tribals. This should be specially made applicable to areas where Primitive Tribal Groups reside.

6.3 Community Control of Non-private Lands

Community control on local natural resources is one of the most significant steps that could help change the situation. Based on the Section 71(4) of the Orissa Panchayat Act, 1964, all wastelands and protected forests within the village should be brought under the control of the Gram Sabha. This needs to be implemented in Scheduled Areas and the Palli Sabha should be given management control of all the land that is not private land.

6.4 Forest Land

The Forest Rights Act 2006 also provides an opportunity for

claiming tribal rights on forest land, both for individual households and on a community basis. The Act explicitly addresses the issue of shifting cultivation on forest land as well as community claims on forests. This needs to be strictly implemented on a priority basis.

6.5 Ancestral Homelands for Primitive Tribal Groups

The land settlement processes in PTG areas have been carried out on the same lines as in any other part of the state. This has left the PTGs extremely vulnerable and at a disadvantage. The Kadalibadi case illustrates how lack of rights on communal lands has led to land alienation of these extremely vulnerable sections. A similar situation exists for Chuktia Bhunjias and Kutia Kondhs, whose ancestral areas have been declared as Sunabeda Wildlife Sanctuary and Kotgarh Sanctuary respectively, where they have no rights on forests or its produce or on their traditional swidden lands. The Dongaria Kondhs are threatened by mining of their most sacred mountain, the Niyamgiri hill, for bauxite. The PTGs generally live in the most remote areas, very rich in forests and water, and which often are the source of major river systems. It is essential to protect both the unique culture of these PTGs and their habitat. Legislation on the lines of recognising ancestral domains of indigenous people in other countries, or on the lines of laws applicable in the north-east, which confer rights communities over all land within their ancestral areas, may be considered for the PTGs.

In the meantime, a strong policy decision must be taken to stop all transfer, alienation or acquisition of land in their ancestral area. This restriction should also include transfer of land categorised as government land, as most of the customary land in the homelands of PTGs has been settled as government land. Land owned by non-PTGs within these areas could be purchased or acquired and distributed to the PTGs on community or individual basis. No new forest lands of any type should be declared in PTG areas.

6.6 Displacement in Scheduled Areas

The issue of displacement in Scheduled Areas needs to be revisited, specially in view of the pre-existing situation arising out of poor settlement of rights of tribals on land. The various cases and examples cited in the study show how the state itself has violated protection of tribal rights in land as provided in Schedule V of the Constitution. To allow large-scale displacement in Scheduled Areas, given the constitutional protection on land, needs to be questioned. It is suggested that instead of diluting the law, the spirit of the *Samata* judgment and the Fifth Schedule of the Constitution be followed and all land transfers in Scheduled Areas to non-tribals be forbidden.

However, all these steps require a strong political will and receptive administrative support. Given that tribals are a minority, with little political voice, it is difficult to visualise that such initiatives will be taken up by the Government of Orissa unless the tribal communities themselves organise to seek their rights.

Bibliography

1. Behuria, N.C., 1965. *Final Report on the Major Settlement Operation in Koraput District, 1938-64*, Board of Revenue, Government of Orissa.
2. Dash, S.N., 2001. *A Study of the Problem of Land Alienation in Tribal Areas with Special Reference to the District of Koraput*, Utkal University, Bhubaneswar.
3. GOI, Planning Commission., 1986. *Report of the Study Group on Land Holding Systems in Tribal Areas*, Planning Commission, New Delhi,.
4. GOO, 1959. *Forest Enquiry Report*, Government of Orissa Press, Cuttack.
5. GOO, 1995. *A Decade of Forestry*, Orissa Forest Department, Govt of Orissa, Bhubaneswar.
6. GOO, 1999. *Revised Working Plan for Nowrangpur Division*, Orissa Forest Department, Cuttack.
7. Haan and Dubey, 2003. *Extreme Deprivation in Remote Areas in India: Social Exclusion as Explanatory Concept*, Paper presented at the 'International Conference on Staying Poor: Chronic Poverty and Development Policy', IDPM, University of Manchester, Manchester, 7 to 9 April 2003. http://idpm.man.ac.uk/cprc/Conference/ conferencepapers/ Dehaan% 20Arjan%20-dubey%2007.03.03.pdf
8. Mahapatra, L.K., 1965. *From Shifting Cultivation to Agriculturist: The Pauri-Bhuiyan in Transition*, Adibasi, October.
9. Mearns, Robin and Saurav Sinha., 1998. *Social Exclusion and Land Administration in Orissa, India*. World Bank, Washington,

10. Ota, Akhil B., 2001. *Reconstructing Livelihood of the Displaced Families in Development Projects: Causes of Failure and Room for Reconstruction*, Anthrobase. Available online at: http://www.anthrobase.com/txt/O/Ota_A_02.htm
11. Padel, F., 1995. *The Sacrifice of Human Being : British Rule and the Konds of Orissa*. Delhi, Oxford University Press, New York.
12. Pandey, B., 1998. *Depriving the Underprivileged for Development*, 1st edn. Institute for Socio-Economic Development, Bhubaneswar.
13. Panigrahi. N., 2001. Impact of State Policies on Management of Land Resources in Tribal Areas of Orissa, *Man & Development*, March.
14. Pattnaik, N., 1993. *Swidden Cultivation amongst Two Tribes of Orissa*, CENDERET, Bhubaneswar, SIDA, New Delhi, and ISO/SWEDFOREST, Bhubaneswar.
15. Pati, B., 1993. *Resisting Domination: Peasants, Tribals, and the National Movement in Orissa, 1920-50*. Manohar Publishers & Distributors, New Delhi.
16. Phansalkar, S.J. and Verma, S., 2004. Improving Water Control as a Strategy for Enhancing Tribal Livelihoods, *Economic and Political Weekly*, July 31.
17. Ramdhyani, R.K., 1947. *Report on Land Tenures and Revenue Systems or Orissa and Chhattisgarh State*.
18. Rath, B., 2005. *Vulnerable Tribal Livelihood and Shifting Cultivation: The Situation in Orissa with a Case Study in the Bhuyan-Juang Pirh of Keonjhar District*, Vasundhara, Bhubaneswar.
19. Rout, S., 1998. *Tribal Land Alienation in Orissa*, Unpublished Report, Indian Social Institute, New Delhi.
20. Sundarajan, S., 1963. *Final Report on the Survey and Settlement of the Kashipur, Karlapat, Mahulpatna and Madanpur-Rampur Ex-Zemindaries in the District of Kalahandi*. Orissa Government Press Cuttack.
21. Thangam, E.S., 1984. *Agro-forestry in Shifting Cultivation Control Programmes in India* in *Social, Economic, and Institutional Aspects of Agroforestry*. Jackson, J.K. and United Nations University Tokyo, Japan.
22. THRTI, 1987. *The Study of Tribal Land Alienation*, Tribal and Harijan Research and Training Institute, GOO, Bhubaneswar.
23. Viegas, P., 1991. *Encroached and Enslaved: Alienation of Tribal Lands and Its Dynamics*. Indian Social Institute, New Delhi.